APR 08 2015

9781482420029

FANTASTIC SCIENCE JOURNEYS

A TRIP THROUGH A CORAL REEF

BY HEATHER MOORE NIVER

Gareth Stevens
PUBLISHING

Please visit our website, www.garethstevens.com. For a free color catalog of all our high-quality books, call toll free 1-800-542-2595 or fax 1-877-542-2596.

Library of Congress Cataloging-in-Publication Data

Niver, Heather Moore.
A trip through a coral reef / by Heather Moore Niver.
p. cm. — (Fantastic science journeys)
Includes index.
ISBN 978-1-4824-2002-9 (pbk.)
ISBN 978-1-4824-2001-2 (6-pack)
ISBN 978-1-4824-2003-6 (library binding)
1. Coral reefs and islands — Juvenile literature. 2. Coral reef ecology — Juvenile literature. I. Niver, Heather Moore. II. Title.
GB461.N58 2015
578.77—d23

First Edition

Published in 2015 by
Gareth Stevens Publishing
111 East 14th Street, Suite 349
New York, NY 10003

Copyright © 2015 Gareth Stevens Publishing

Designer: Sarah Liddell
Editor: Ryan Nagelhout

Photo credits: Cover, p. 1 Borisoff/Shutterstock.com; pp. 5, 11, 19, 29 Ethan Daniels/Shutterstock.com; p. 7 Vlad61/Shutterstock.com; p. 9 (main) C.K.Ma/Shutterstock.com; pp. 9 (polyp), 13 Sphinx Wang/Shutterstock.com; p. 15 Rich Carey/Shutterstock.com; p. 17 deb22/Shutterstock.com; p. 21 Greg Johnston/Lonely Planet Images/Getty Images; p. 23 (background) Dudarev Mikhail/Shutterstock.com; p. 23 (butterfly fish) Sergey Skleznev/Shutterstock.com; p. 23 (surgeon fish and cleaner wrass) Nantawat Chotsuwan/Shutterstock.com; p. 23 (puffer) Beth Swanson/Shutterstock.com; p. 23 (grouper) Leonardo Gonzalez/Shutterstock.com; p. 23 (parrotfish) Cigdem Sean Cooper/Shutterstock.com; p. 25 Off Axis Production/Shutterstock.com; p. 27 (main) Luis Javier Sandoval/Oxford Scientific/Getty Images; p. 27 (coral farm) Laurentiu Garofeanu/Barcroft Media/Getty Images.

All rights reserved. No part of this book may be reproduced in any form without permission in writing from the publisher, except by a reviewer.

Printed in the United States of America

CPSIA compliance information: Batch #CW15GS: For further information contact Gareth Stevens, New York, New York at 1-800-542-2595.

CONTENTS

It's Alive! 4
Let's Look for Coral Reefs 6
Underwater Buddies 8
Pointy and Poisonous! 10
Crazy Colors 12
The Right Stuff 14
Brief Reef History 16
Forming a Fringing Reef 18
Building a Barrier Reef and Atoll 20
Reef Beasts 22
Medical Miracles in the Reefs 24
Coral Farms and Reef Balls 26
Caring for Coral Reefs 28
Glossary 30
For More Information 31
Index 32

Words in the glossary appear in **bold** type the first time they are used in the text.

IT'S ALIVE!

Coral reefs look like colorful rock gardens in the ocean. Coral reefs are formed of small sea animals. They're always growing and changing.

Corals are tiny animals with soft bodies. They form a hard, cup-shaped outer **skeleton** and stick to the ocean floor, where they live all their life. After they die and their body breaks down, their skeleton remains. Over a long time, these skeletons build up and form reefs.

Want a closer look? Imagine you can shrink down and climb into a tiny ship. Let's explore a coral reef!

THAT'S FANTASTIC!
A coral's skeleton can be internal— inside its body— or external, which means outside its body. The corals that make reefs have external skeletons.

Sometimes coral reefs are called rainforests of the sea.

LET'S LOOK FOR CORAL REEFS

We can't dive just anywhere and find coral reefs. The best place to find them is along the **equator**. Reefs commonly form near the equator along ocean shores.

Look for shallow water less than 300 feet (90 m) deep. Search for clear water, too. This water won't have too many nutrients in it. Lots of nutrients make water cloudy so sunlight can't shine through. Corals need sunlight to live and grow.

THAT'S FANTASTIC!

Corals belong to the same animal group as sea anemones (uh-NEH-muh-neez) and jellyfish. Sea anemones are ocean animals that look like flowers.

Many different animals call coral reefs home.

UNDERWATER BUDDIES

Coral **polyps** and **algae** called zooxanthellae (zoh-uh-zaan-THEH-lee) are good buddies. They have a **symbiotic** relationship. This means they help each other out. Zooxanthellae live inside the polyp and take in sunlight through its see-through body. The polyp gives them a safe place to live.

Algae make food by using sunlight and a gas called carbon dioxide. This is called **photosynthesis**. They share this food with the coral. Zooxanthellae get a place to live, and the coral gets food.

THAT'S FANTASTIC!
If coral build up in water that's too shallow, they can dry out and die. They're also in danger of being harmed during storms.

Without the zooxanthellae making food, the reefs would not have their bright colors.

polyp

zooxanthellae

POINTY AND POISONOUS!

Most corals get their food delivered by algae's photosynthesis, but they can also get dinner themselves. Corals have pointy, poisonous **tentacles** they can stick out to grab some tasty treats that might be floating by. They usually strike for dinner at night. Our ship stays away from the tentacles and keeps us safe.

A coral's tentacles have special stinging cells called nematocysts (nih-MAA-toh-sihsts). They sting like a jellyfish! Corals' most common meal is zooplankton, which are the tiniest animals on Earth.

THAT'S FANTASTIC!
Sometimes, maybe when they're very hungry, corals can snag small fish. The poison in their tentacles can be deadly!

Coral tentacles also keep other bits of matter away from the polyp.

CRAZY COLORS

Corals come in all kinds of crazy colors. All these wild colors come from the algae living in the coral.

Our ship has found some coral without color. Just like people, corals can get stressed out. Corals lose their color because they lose the zooxanthellae living in them when they're stressed. Things like big temperature changes and pollution stress out corals. Corals will also lose their color if they're removed from the water.

THAT'S FANTASTIC!

The crown-of-thorns starfish likes to eat living coral so much that it has destroyed some of the Great Barrier Reef. Fish, worms, and snails also munch on polyps.

The Great Barrier Reef near Australia is the biggest reef system in the world.

THE RIGHT STUFF

Corals come in all different shapes and sizes. Some look like plants or leaves. Brain coral gets its name because it looks like a human brain! Soft coral and deep-water coral can live in water colder than 70°F (21°C).

Only a certain kind of coral can form a reef. Reefs are formed from hard, or stony, shallow-water coral. Common kinds of hard coral include brain, mushroom, pillar, staghorn, and plate (or table) coral.

THAT'S FANTASTIC!

The movement of the water makes the different coral shapes. For example, strong waves make thick or flat coral shapes.

The Great Barrier Reef is made up of more than 350 different species, or kinds, of coral.

brain coral

15

BRIEF REEF HISTORY

About 500 million years ago, supertiny animals called coral polyps lived in some **tropical** waters. They stuck themselves to the ocean floor near the shoreline. The first reefs were born.

There are three main kinds of coral reefs. Fringing reefs are most common and form along the shore. Barrier reefs grow farther out from shore. The third type of reef is called an atoll. The Great Barrier Reef started forming around the end of the last ice age, about 10,000 years ago.

THAT'S FANTASTIC!
The Great Barrier Reef covers more than 135,000 square miles (350,000 sq km) and runs 1,250 miles (2,000 km) from north to south near northeastern Australia.

The Great Barrier Reef is along the northern coast of Australia.

FORMING A FRINGING REEF

Reefs form when one polyp attaches to the ocean floor. That polyp buds, or divides, into thousands of **clones**. These new polyps attach to one another and form a colony. Little by little, more and more colonies join and build up into a reef.

A reef along the shore of a continent or island is called a fringing reef. If coral has light, shallow water, and their good pals the zooxanthellae, the fringing reef will slowly get bigger and bigger.

THAT'S FANTASTIC!

The Great Barrier Reef isn't just one reef. More than 2,900 smaller reefs make up this amazing reef system!

From our ship, we see the result of millions of years of coral reef building.

BUILDING A BARRIER REEF AND ATOLL

Over time as sea levels rise, the land where the fringing reef started growing sinks. A **lagoon** slowly forms next to it and separates the land from the reef to make a barrier reef. It's a long, thin strip that runs along the shoreline. Most of it is underwater.

If sea levels keep rising and falling, the land near the reef may sink so that only the reef can be seen at the surface of the water. Now the barrier reef has become an atoll.

THAT'S FANTASTIC!

Some barrier reefs and atolls can take from 100,000 to 300,000 years to build up, depending on how big they are!

The Belize Barrier Reef is the second-largest barrier reef in the world. It has been named a UNESCO World Heritage site.

REEF BEASTS

Our ship passes many animals swimming around the reef! Reefs are an important source of shelter for animals. Seabirds, sponges, jellyfish, and starfish call coral reefs home, along with shrimp, rays, snails, crabs, lobsters, sea turtles, and sea snakes.

Coral reefs make up only 1 percent of the ocean floor, but 25 percent of the ocean's animals call those reefs home! Experts think millions of kinds of animals in reefs have yet to be discovered!

THAT'S FANTASTIC!
More than 200 kinds of birds and 1,500 kinds of fish live near the Great Barrier Reef.

REEF FISH

Scientists divide reef fish into six major groups based on how they get their food:

GROUP	FISH EXAMPLES	FEEDING
planktivores 	groupers, butterfly fish, damselfish	feed in large schools, or groups; feed on plankton found near coral reef
herbivores 	surgeon fish	eat algae growing on reef
omnivores 	triggerfish, puffers	eat **crustaceans** and reef algae
piscivores 	groupers	eat other fish around reef
invertebrate predators 	parrot fish	eat coral polyps and other **invertebrates**
cleaner fish 	cleaner wrass	eat mucus and parasites found on the skin of other fishes

MEDICAL MIRACLES IN THE REEFS

Besides being home to so many animals, coral reefs are an important part of the medical world. By studying the incredible range of life in coral reefs, scientists have found or are working on drugs for cancer, infections, viruses, and much more.

Coral reefs are also a form of protection for land and humans. They keep waves from eroding, or wearing down, land. Reefs also protect harbors, wetlands, and property.

THAT'S FANTASTIC!

More than half a billion people live within about 60 miles (100 km) of a coral reef.

The coral reefs in the Florida Keys bring in millions of people every year. These visitors contribute about $7.6 billion to the economy!

CORAL FARMS AND REEF BALLS

We want to keep our planet's coral reefs healthy. Reefs are an important part of ocean life, and humans have learned how to help reefs grow. At coral farms, polyps are grown and then planted on a healthy reef. The Nature Conservancy has farms off the coast of Florida and in the Virgin Islands that grow coral.

New reefs can also be started on "reef balls." These are hollow balls like bubbles made of concrete. They are made to draw coral polyps and other ocean animals.

THAT'S FANTASTIC!

There are 5,000 reef balls already growing coral around the world in more than 59 countries.

Reef balls and coral farms help new coral grow all over the world.

coral farm

27

CARING FOR CORAL REEFS

Now that we've explored coral reefs, we know we need to help keep them healthy. Stressed coral will kick out the algae. If the stress isn't fixed somehow, the coral will die. Pollution, disease, people, and warming waters are just some of the dangers to coral reefs.

Our fantastic field trip through the reefs has ended. These reefs are both beautiful and priceless to humans and animals. We should all be careful when swimming or boating near these important reefs. Let's help them live for millions more years!

THAT'S FANTASTIC!
Corals sense changes in the weather. Scientists can even use coral reef fossils to learn about the weather millions of years ago.

The area north of Australia is often called the Coral Triangle. More than 600 kinds of coral grow there.

GLOSSARY

algae: plantlike living things that are mostly found in water

clone: an exact copy of an animal

crustacean: an animal with a hard shell that lives in water

equator: an imaginary line around Earth that is the same distance from the North and South Poles

invertebrate: an animal without a backbone

lagoon: water between the shore and a coral reef

photosynthesis: the process used by plants and algae to make food from sunlight and carbon dioxide

polyp: a single coral animal

skeleton: the strong frame that supports an animal's body

symbiotic: having to do with a relationship in which two parties live together and help one another to live

tentacle: a long, thin body part that sticks out from an animal's head or mouth

tropical: having to do with the warm parts of Earth near the equator

FOR MORE INFORMATION

BOOKS

George, Lynn. *Coral: Reef Builders*. New York, NY: PowerKids Press, 2010.

Schomp, Virginia. *24 Hours on a Coral Reef*. New York, NY: Marshall Cavendish, 2013.

Simon, Seymour. *Coral Reefs*. New York, NY: Harper, 2013.

WEBSITES

Coral Reef
kids.nceas.ucsb.edu/biomes/coralreef.html
Dive in for all kinds of coral reefs, the animals that call them home, and more!

NOAA Coral Reef Conservation Program
coralreef.noaa.gov/
Learn all about coral, coral reefs, and what we can do to protect them.

Publisher's note to educators and parents: Our editors have carefully reviewed these websites to ensure that they are suitable for students. Many websites change frequently, however, and we cannot guarantee that a site's future contents will continue to meet our high standards of quality and educational value. Be advised that students should be closely supervised whenever they access the Internet.

INDEX

algae 8, 10, 12, 23, 28
atoll 16, 20
barrier reefs 16, 20
Belize Barrier Reef 21
clones 18
colony 18
colors 9, 12
coral farms 26, 27
Coral Triangle 29
drugs 24
equator 6
food 8, 9, 10, 23
fringing reefs 16, 18, 20
Great Barrier Reef 12, 13, 15, 16, 17, 18
hard coral 14
nematocysts 10
photosynthesis 8, 10
polyps 8, 11, 12, 16, 18, 23, 26
reef animals 7, 22, 23
reef balls 26
shapes 14
skeleton 4
species 15
stress 12, 28
symbiotic relationship 8
tentacles 10, 11
zooplankton 10
zooxanthellae 8, 9, 12, 18